Children's Word Games and Crossword Puzzles

For Ages 7 to 9
Edited by Eugene T. Maleska

Random House
Puzzles & Games

Copyright © 1986 by Eugene T. Maleska

All rights reserved under International and Pan-American Copyright Conventions.
Published in the United States by Random House, Inc., New York,
and simultaneously in Canada by Random House of Canada Limited, Toronto.

Random House is a registered trademark of Random House, Inc.

Library of Congress Cataloging-in-Publication Data
Maleska, Eugene T.
    Children's word games and crossword puzzles.
    Summary: A collection of thirty-five original
crossword puzzles and word games for players aged
seven to nine.
    1. Crossword puzzles—Juvenile literature.
2. Word games—Juvenile literature. [1. Crossword
puzzles. 2. Word games] I. Title.
GV1507.C7M3431986   793.73'2   86-888
ISBN 0-8129-3521-7

Manufactured in the United States of America

10 9 8 7 6 5 4 3 2 1

Woodcut illustrations by Lars and Lois Hokanson

1.
Easy Words
by Susan Brown

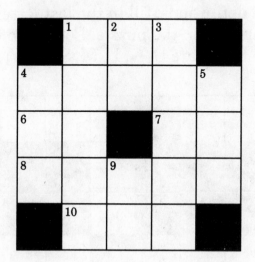

Across

1 When you do a good deed, you get a ____ on the back

4 A comedian has a good sense of ____

6 Opposite of down

7 You and I

8 Weary

10 Was first in line

Down

1 A child in class, or part of your eye

2 Jack Horner said: "What a good boy ____ I!"

3 When a car breaks down, it may need to be ____ away

4 Shack

5 Bright color in the U.S. flag

9 Do, ____, mi

2.
Ha Ha
by Merryl Maleska

Using the definitions, fill in the last letter in each word and also fill in the puzzle. Letters to use somewhere below are D, G, L, M, S, T, W, and Y.

Across

1 What you wear on your head   HA __

2 "Mary ___ a little lamb"   HA __

3 Witch   HA __

4 Computer in the movie called *2001*   HA __

Down

1 Meat from a pig   HA __

2 Food for horses   HA __

3 Owns   HA __

4 *Hee* ___ is a funny TV program   HA __

3.
Picture Puzzle
by Walter Covell

What goes in box 1, 2, 3, 4, and 5: B, C, H, R, or V?

1 | A T

2 | A T

3 | A T

4 | A T

5 | A T

4.
Fun and 8-Across

by Peter G. Snow

Across

1 Doctor's degree: Abbreviation

3 "Rain, rain, ____ away"

5 Alley ____ of comics

7 Cupid, McGrew, or Rather

8 Football and baseball, for example

10 Another name for Dad

11 A sour yellow fruit

13 This may be made of steel or chocolate

14 Place to take a bath

16 Cry of pain

17 ____ Cobb was a great baseball player

Down

1 Abbreviation for Missouri

2 A pet that barks

3 Fuel for an automobile

4 Opposite of off

6 Something to write on

7 Train or bus station

9 What you might call your mother

11 What policemen enforce

12 Pecan or crazy person

13 ___ Derek is a famous actress

15 Word that sounds like buy

5.
Ho! Ho!
by Merryl Maleska

Using the definitions, fill in the missing letters in each word and also fill in the puzzle.

Across

1 Opposite of cold   HO __

2 Relative of a pig   HO __

4 What person?   __ HO

5 This is worn over your
sock   __ HO __

9 A tramp is called a ____   HO __ __

10 A snapshot taken with
a camera   __ HO __ __

Down

1 Animal a jockey rides   HO __ __ __

2 In what way?   HO __

3 Tool used by a
gardener   HO __

6 Sound made by an owl   HO __ __

7 What a bricklayer
carries   HO __

8 What do rabbits do?   HO __

6.
Picture Puzzle
by Louis Sabin

What four-letter word can you find by adding and subtracting the words that the pictures stand for?

The pictures are the key to the answer!

7.
All Kinds of Animals
by Louis Sabin

As you fill the list of words into the puzzle, cross them off one by one. To give you a start, two words have been filled in.

3 letters	**4 letters**	**5 letters**	**6 letters**	**7 letters**
elk	bats	frogs	rabbit	cheetah
hen	bees	hippo		turkeys
pig	calf	shark		parrots
	cats			
	fish			

8.
Stairway of Words
by Bernice Gordon

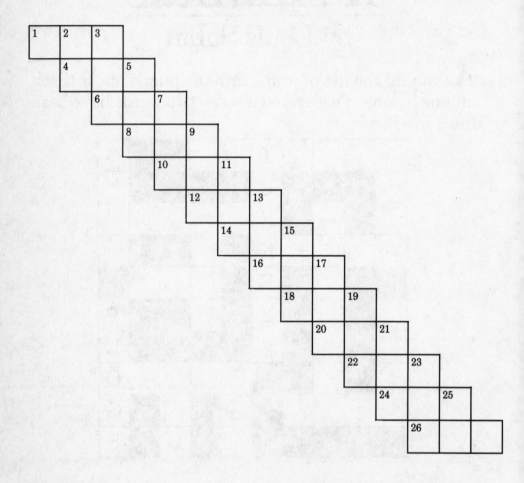

Across

1 Had a meal

4 "____, two, buckle my shoe"

6 This stops up the water in a river

8 What you do when you use oars

10 This looks like a needle

12 This makes the cars run

14 "____ goes the weasel!"

16 Not dry

18 This covers roofs or roads

20 "I've ___ sixpence"

22 A poodle or a collie

24 Small, strong boat that pulls ships

26 Lots of people, or maybe a gang

Down

2 "Happy Birthday ___ You"

3 Finish

5 What you hear with

7 Something you use to clean the floor

9 Covering for a bald head or any other head

11 Take a ___ (sleep for a short time)

13 Mother of a piglet

15 A canary or a kitten

17 Game played in the school yard

19 Pole used by a fisherman

21 Little child

23 Some people chew bubble ___

25 "Get ready; get set; ___!"

9.
A Nice Mixture
by Peter G. Snow

Across

1 As wise as ___ owl

3 Word of greeting

5 Cut the grass on a lawn

7 What Jack Sprat couldn't eat

8 TV knobs

10 A common dessert

11 A four-door car

13 Angry or crazy

14 What Miss Muffet did

16 ___ Asner is a famous actor

17 Leave or depart

Down

1 Opposite of P.M.

2 Companion of Wynken and Blynken

3 Owns or possesses

4 In the game of tag, one person is _____

6 Cleaned a windshield

7 Insects that bother dogs

9 Help or assist

11 Unhappy

12 Pester (also an old horse)

13 Abbreviation for Maine

15 "I pledge allegiance _____ the flag"

10.
A Tree of Words
by Bernice Gordon

Across

1 Enemy

4 Hasten

6 Two thousand pounds

7 ___, white and blue

9 Naughty

10 Uncle ___ of the U.S.A.

12 Droop

13 Cow's sound

15 Hound or Great Dane

16 Happy puppies ___ their tails

18 In what way?

19 Present from Santa

Down

1 What children have during recess

2 Take it ___ leave it

3 Make a mistake

4 What a mason carries

5 Opposite of no

6 Playground game

8 A water barrier

9 Container for groceries

11 Cut the grass

12 Female pig

14 Horse's morsel

15 "___ unto others . . ."

17 "___ fly a kite!"

11.
Go! Go!
by Merryl Maleska

Using the definitions, fill in the missing letters in each word and also fill in the puzzle.

Across

1 A bell that rings in a school or firehouse
GO __ __

4 "No news is ___ news"
GO __ __

5 Extreme pain
__ GO __ __

7 What scuba divers wear over their eyes
GO __ __ __ __ __

9 Become rotten, as an egg (2 words)
GO __ __ __

13 ___ *with the Wind* is a famous book and movie   GO __ __

14 "As I was ___ to Saint Ives . . ."   GO __ __ __

15 "Thursday's child has far ___" (2 words)
__ __   GO

Down

1 These animals are related to sheep
GO __ __ __

2 A boat in Venice or a freight car
GO __ __ __ __ __

3 "Do unto others as you would have them do unto you" is the ___ rule   GO __ __ __ __

6 Cavemen lived long, long ___
__ GO

8 Didn't remember
__ __ __ GO __

10 San ___ is the home of the Padres and the Chargers
__ __ __ GO

11 The ___ Desert is in Asia   GO __ __

12 A gambling game played with numbers and cards
__ __ __ GO

19

12.
A Young Man of Words

by Bert Rosenfield

Across

1 Had breakfast

4 Finish first in a race

7 A kind of soup

8 The highest card in the deck

9 Sharp part of a knife

11 Sometimes you have it for dinner

12 A note that follows "so"

13 "___ called for his pipe"

14 It's on the end of a pencil

17 First note of the scale

18 I ___ working on a puzzle

19 It takes pictures

23 Big ___ an elephant

24 A short name for Alan

25 Shut one eye

27 A toy that spins

30 Two ___ two makes four

31 This very minute

32 You see it when you look up while outside

33 Sheep that sounds like "you"

Down

1 Animal like King Kong

2 A shorter name for Teddy

3 Big American bird

4 What we swim in

5 What 4 Down is when it freezes

6 Not used at all

10 What you hear with

11 "___ sells sea shells ..."

15 He was the first man

16 Just a few

19 A sweet treat

20 "May I ___ a question?"

21 A sunbeam

22 A hermit lives ___

25 "There ___ a crooked man"

26 It comes out of a pen

28 What you say when your hair gets pulled

29 You must pay back what you ___

13.
Double Meanings
by Walter Covell

Each of the words below goes into 2 blanks on the opposite page.

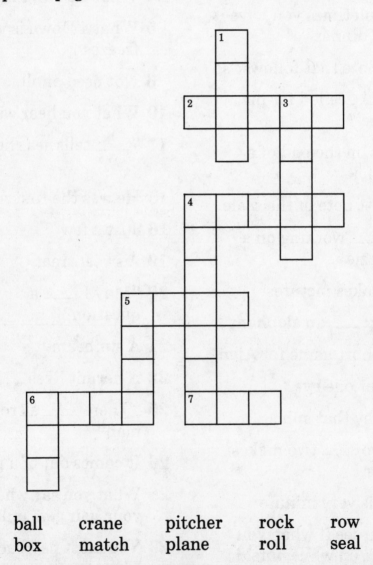

ball   crane   pitcher   rock   row
box   match   plane   roll   seal

Pour water from a ＿＿＿
(4 Down).

A pilot flies a ＿＿＿
(4 Across).

A mail ＿＿＿ holds letters
(6 Down).

A carpenter makes wood
smooth with a ＿＿＿
(4 Across).

One way to start a fire is to
strike a ＿＿＿ (2 Across).

A baby may sleep if you
＿＿＿ its cradle (5 Across).

Mary's garden has pretty
maids all in a ＿＿＿
(7 Across).

Some skates slide on ice.
Others ＿＿＿ on the ground
(5 Down).

You need a ＿＿＿ to play
soccer or tennis (6 Across).

With flippers, a ＿＿＿ can
swim in water or walk on
land (1 Down).

People who ＿＿＿ should
wear gloves (6 Down).

The ＿＿＿ throws a baseball
to the catcher (4 Down).

You can lick the flap of an
envelope to ＿＿＿ it
(1 Down).

Cinderella lost her slipper
at the ＿＿＿ (6 Across).

Things that ＿＿＿ look alike
(2 Across).

The Pilgrims landed on
Plymouth ＿＿＿ (5 Across).

A ＿＿＿ is a kind of bread
(5 Down).

A ＿＿＿ has long legs and
wades in shallow water
(3 Down).

You lift heavy things with a
＿＿＿ (3 Down).

With oars you can ＿＿＿ a
boat (7 Across).

14.
Cars

by Bernice Gordon

Using the definitions, finish the ten cars below.

1 Food for Bugs Bunny

2 Sliced the turkey

3 Here's Johnny!: TV star

4 Famous opera

5 Hug or fondle

6 Rug

7 President before Reagan

8 Profession; occupation

9 Black paper used by typists

10 Christmas songs

1	C	A	R			
2	C	A	R			
3	C	A	R			
4	C	A	R			
5	C	A	R			
6	C	A	R			
7	C	A	R			
8	C	A	R			
9	C	A	R			
10	C	A	R			

24

15.
Here, Kitty, Kitty!

by Bert Rosenfield

Across

1 Another name for Daddy

5 A skunk has a bad ____

6 "Please ____ your seat"

7 "Take ____ Out to the Ball Game"

8 An insect that rhymes with plant

11 The bottom of your shoe

15 This is a part of your house

17 Opposite of bright

18 A short way of writing Mister

19 Big mountains in South America

21 "Have you ____ wool?"

22 A ____ on the back means "good work"

24 Not early

28 Ginger ____ (a bubbly drink)

29 Leave something out

30 What you say when you don't want any

31 Something that holds your paddle back

32 What two people play on the piano

34 How to spell the last letter in the alphabet

36 Put 3 and 2 together to make 5

37 A houseplant that has to be watered

38 What you say when you meet a friend

39 Joan of ____ was a famous French saint

41 Breakfast is one, and so is dinner

43 A note that follows "la"

(Continued)

44 ____ pop (a drink)

47 Sometimes you take one during the day

48 Do, ____, mi

49 Letters that follow Js

Down

1 What you cook things in

2 He lived in the Garden of Eden

3 Sticks a finger in your ribs

4 "Stay where you ____!"

8 Your hand is at the end of your ____

9 If it's red, it's neither black ____ white

10 A word that sounds like "two"

12 ____ or even

13 Something you should not tell

14 They follow el's

16 A boy after he grows up

20 What some stockings are made of

21 Had lunch

22 Black-and-white animal in the zoo

23 Sometimes the class has to read ____

25 Really surprise

26 A big animal with stripes

27 A movie about a visitor from space

31 A short way of writing "street"

33 This is a nickname for Edward

35 When you come in, you —ter

37 Something that water puts out

38 It makes a nice sandwich

40 Pets that sometimes scratch (see the picture!)

42 A big animal that roars

45 How it looks when the lights are out

46 Animals that swing in the trees

16.
Get the Pictures
by Louis Sabin

Clue: Don't catch one, 'cause it's not so hot to have one!

Rearrange these letters to find something you shouldn't catch.

17.
Find the State
by Merryl Maleska

A state in the United States is the answer to this puzzle. Insert the correct words next to their clues; then put the numbered letters on the numbered blanks below.

candles	born	batter	fifteen	closet
meal	minutes	March	chicken	

There are sixty in one hour   __ __ __ __ __ __ __

5

The month after February   __ __ __ __ __

9

If he's lucky, he hits a home run   __ __ __ __ __ __

8

You were ___ on your birthday   __ __ __ __

7

A girl or boy who just turned nine would have to blow out nine ___!   __ __ __ __ __ __ __

3

A good place to hang your clothes   __ __ __ __ __ __

6

It comes out of an egg   __ __ __ __ __ __ __

2

The number after fourteen   __ __ __ __ __ __ __

4

Breakfast, lunch, or dinner   __ __ __ __

1

Answer: __ __ __ __ __ __ __ __ __

1   2   3   4   5   6   7   8   9

29

18.
No! No!

by Merryl Maleska

Using the definitions, fill in the missing letters in each word and also fill in the puzzle.

Across

1 What you tie on a rope or string

__ NO __

4 What skiers glide on

__ NO __

6 This is a shortened word for an office girl

__ __ __ NO

8 This boat is used by Indians and campers

__ __ NO __

11 A word that sounds exactly like "no" __ NO __

12 What Mother Hubbard's poor dog had   NO __ __

14 Carolers sing this word at Christmas NO __ __

Down

2 Do, re, and mi are ____ in a scale   NO __ __ __

3 A man whose singing voice is high is called a ____   __ __ NO __

5 This person moves about from place to place in search of food NO __ __ __

7 At a football game the crowd makes a lot of ____   NO __ __ __

9 Pinocchio's ____ grew every time he told a lie NO __ __

10 The loop on a cowboy's rope is called a ____ NO __ __ __

11 The handle on a door or drawer is called a ____ __ NO __

13 The present time NO __

19.
Some Famous People

by Peter G. Snow

Across

1 You can buy stamps ____ the post office

3 "____ stuck a feather in his cap"

5 What little George Washington couldn't tell

7 Opposite of good

8 King with a golden touch

10 ____ Grissom was a famous astronaut

11 Belonging to them

13 _____ Carney is a famous actor

14 Woman who lives in a convent

16 "Where are you going, _____ pretty maid?"

17 "Ride a cockhorse _____ Banbury Cross"

Down

1 _____ Pacino is a famous actor

2 Tiny _____ is a boy in a Christmas story

3 Owns

4 Nickname for Edward

6 Number between seven and nine

7 Place to wash one's face

9 Owed, like a debt

11 "_____ it, you'll like it"

12 Something that makes a road rough

13 Willy Boy said: "I _____ going to the meadows"

15 "Jack Sprat could eat _____ fat"

20.
Words That Sound Alike

by Walter Covell

What words fit in the blanks and the grid?

bear	coal	deer	hare	heal
bare	cole	dear	hair	heel
pear	reed	sees	steak	tale
pair	read	seas	stake	tail

14 Across. Say, did you never ever ____

14 Down. That some grass is a kind of ____?

9 Across. While tied up to a wooden ____,

12 Down. A dog was eating T-bone ____!

10 Across. Down from the tree there fell one ____,

10 Down. And then a second made a ____!

3 Down. The world is round, the spaceman ____,

11 Across. Flying over lands and ____!

7 Down. Now, when the tortoise beat the ____,

2 Down. Did he win by just a ____?

4 Down. That merry old soul, King ____,

4 Across. Did not fill his pipe with ____!

6 Down. His mother, Mrs. ____,

16 Across. Always called Bambi, "____"!

5 Across. When Mother Hubbard found the cupboard ____,

8 Across. Perhaps the bone was stolen by a ____!

1 Across. If you fall down and hurt your ____,

1 Down. Cheer up, in time it's sure to ____!

15 Across. Have you ever heard a ____

13 Across. Shorter than a monkey's ____?

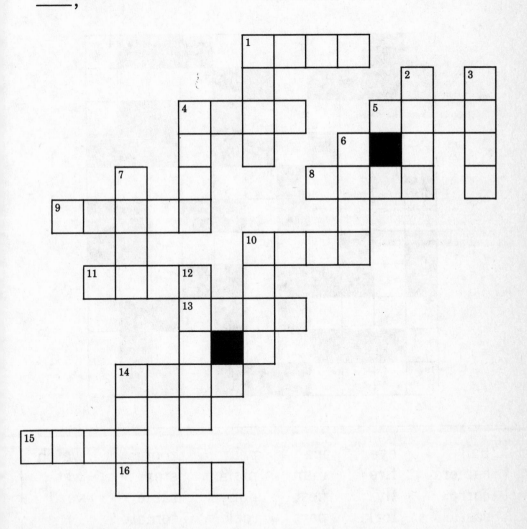

35

21.
Fill-In Puzzle
by James and Phyllis Barrick

As you fill the words into the puzzle, cross them off in the box beneath the diagram.

ball	eye	ice	pear	room	watch
camera	fire	man	piano	star	wet
carrot	fly	nest	pony	table	yard
castle	fork	paw	rock	tomato	

Across

2 At dinnertime, the family sits around the ___

5 Small horse

6 House for a princess

8 Animal's foot

10 Orange vegetable

12 Playing with matches can cause a ___

13 Spaghetti is often served with ___ sauce

14 The ___ in the moon

16 Eating utensil

18 Timepiece often worn on a person's wrist

19 Three feet

Down

1 ___ 'n' roll

3 What a bowler rolls

4 Organ of sight

5 "And a partridge in a ___ tree"

7 It twinkles at night

8 Instrument with 88 keys

9 Soaked

10 What a photographer uses

11 A kitchen, for example

15 Home for sparrows

16 Go up in a plane

17 ___ cream cone

22.
Words You've Heard

by Merryl Maleska

1	2	3		4	5	6
7				8		
9			10			
11						
12	13	14		15	16	17
18						
19				20		
21				22		

Across

1 What is the first name of actor Selleck or pitcher Seaver?

4 What is the opposite of good?

7 Cavemen and dinosaurs lived long, long ____

38

8 What drink did Robin Hood like?

9 When you make a ____ to somebody, you shouldn't break it

11 This person helps to make laws in Washington, D.C.

12 A man who digs trenches is called a ____

18 Doctors who are called surgeons ____ on people

19 What separates the players on a tennis court?

20 When a bee is angry, it uses ____ stinger

21 These letters come after *host*, *steward*, and *count*

22 Preachers often say: "____ us pray"

Down

1 When it's time to go to sleep at camp, the bugler plays ____

2 The monster in a fairy tale is called an ____

3 What did the cow jump over in a nursery rhyme?

4 When you go fishing for flounder, you must use ____ to tempt the fish

5 When you fish, you must ____ have a hook on the end of your line

6 This is an animal like Bambi

10 The head of a city is called the ____

12 Texas is called the ____ Star State

13 These animals were Tarzan's friends

14 People make ____ at a racetrack and often lose their money

15 When you go down a steep stairway, hold on to the ____

16 This is an ending for cigar, major or kitchen

17 What you need when you are tired

23.
Royal People

by June Boggs

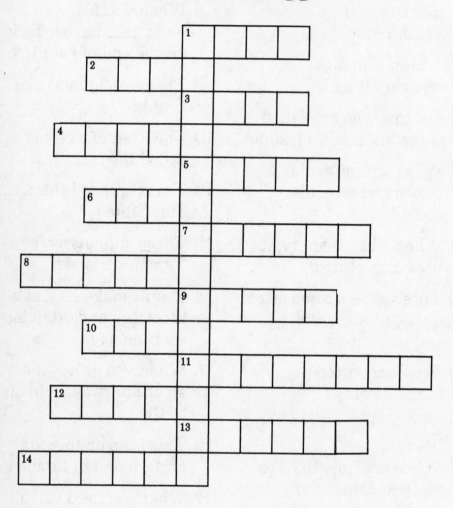

Across

1 Part of a leg

2 Another name for a cab

3 Food for squirrels

4 Bees can do this

5 Sugary

6 Some dolls say this

7 Five cents

8 Used some glue

9 What a duck says

10 Read this in a restaurant

11 Very large animal

12 Dish you eat on

13 Something to add or subtract

14 Playtime at school

Down

1 People who wear crowns (3 words)

24.
Numbers Game
by Peter G. Snow

Across

1 Can you count ___ to 100?

3 Lovable movie character from space

5 A large body of water, like an ocean

7 Number between one and three

8 Stare at with anger

10 Lowest number

11 Finished

13 Honey maker that might sting you

14 Tool for a carpenter

16 An overhead train is called an ___

17 "Bake ___ a cake as fast as you can"

Down

1 "Give ___ this day our daily bread"

2 A nickname for Margaret

3 A female lamb (sounds like "you")

4 Word that sounds like "two"

6 All by one's self

7 Large woody plants in a forest

9 Four ___ four add up to eight

11 Fish that looks like a snake

12 Something that stops up a river

13 "___ my Valentine"

15 "Now ___ Are Six" is a story by A. A. Milne

25.
An OK Puzzle
by Louis Sabin

As you fill in the blank spaces, cross off the words in the box on the opposite page.

#					Clue
1	O	K			All right; yes
2		O	K		Funny story
3		O	K		Jab, with finger or elbow
4		O	K		Roused from sleep
5	O		K		Sturdy trees
6		O		K	Douse with water
7		O		K	Boat's landing place
8		O		K	What a key fits into
9		O		K	Stone or popular music
10		O		K	Short stocking
11		O		K	Yellow part of an egg
12		O		K	Horn sound or goose's cry
13		O		K	Fishline float; bottle stopper
14		O		K	Library item
15		O		K	Meal maker
16		O		K	Captain _____ of *Peter Pan*

sock	cook	woke	cork
poke	okay	hook	joke
oaks	rock	soak	book
yolk	dock	honk	lock

26.
All Around the House
by Walter Covell

When you fill the words into the puzzle, cross them off in the box at the bottom of the opposite page.

Across

3 From the _____, smoke goes up the chimney

6 If you want to sit, head for the nearest _____

7 Bread comes out of a _____ brown and crisp

9 A ___ is a good place to store books

13 People often park their cars in a ___

14 To roast meat, heat up the ___

15 The ___ is the cover for your house

16 After clothes are washed, they can air on the clothesline, or go into a ___.

18 To take a bath, turn on the ___ water

Down

1 If your ___ has too much food on it, you won't be able to eat all of it

2 Hinges on a ___ let it open and shut

3 You can hold meat with a ___ while you cut it with a knife

4 Butter and milk are stored in a ___

5 Mother may use a pan or a ___ to cook with

6 If the bathwater is too hot, turn on the ___ water

8 A good way to eat soup is to use a ___

10 To get water, turn on the ___

11 If you don't have a sharpener, you can sharpen a pencil with a ___

12 Pillows, sheets, and blankets are found on a ___

17 A ___ can save a wooden floor from wear

bed	chair	cold	dish
faucet	fireplace	fork	garage
oven	pot	refrigerator	roof

door	dryer	spoon
hot	knife	toaster
rug	shelf	

47

27.
Game Dog
by Bert Rosenfield

Across

1 "Come on ___"

3 Card higher than a king

4 Irish or English ones

9 What the postman brings

13 It makes you cry when you peel it

15 He comes around on Christmas Eve

16 Not far away

18 Something that you plant

20 What a horse eats

23 What you sometimes call Father

24 A hot drink sometimes made by dipping a bag

25 The first day of the week ____ Sunday

26 You often see Uncle ____ in a July Fourth parade

27 The first letters of New and York

28 If it's mine, it belongs to ____

Down

1 What we skate on

2 It helps in catching a fish

3 As big ____ a house

5 "Bobby Shaftoe went ____ sea"

6 Prefix with courage or roll

7 A kind of pudding

8 Opposite of bought

9 What you sometimes call Mother

10 "Eat ____ apple a day"

11 When you play tag, sometimes you're ____

12 A note that follows "sol"

14 If you don't want any, you say "____ thanks"

15 What they have in buses and trains

17 "She had ____ many children . . ."

18 What yo-yos and tops do

19 Not hard

21 Mets or Yankees or Giants

22 Another word for alike

28.
Fill In the Words

by James and Phyllis Barrick

As you fill the list of words into the puzzle, cross them off one by one. To give you a start, the two longest words have been filled in.

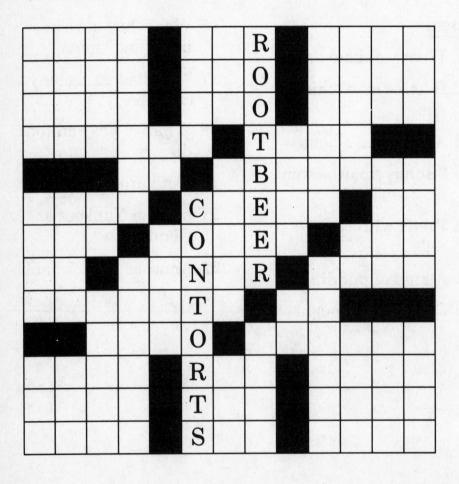

2 Letters

ad
do
ed
it
ma
me
no
so

3 Letters

ago
coo
ego
eye
hen
lad
odd
per
pie
rye
sag
sun
toe
you

4 Letters

ache
care
core
deer
dice
edge
emit
eras
flag
flip
gear
hilt
into
iris
late
less
name
omen
omit
open
pace
peer
rope
rots
sets
tear
teen
they
tied
tone

5 Letters

alley
chord
clean
holes
miner
niece

6 Letters

attain
cancel
ending
manner
stride
tennis

7 Letters

abridge
penalty

8 Letters

contorts
root beer

51

29.
Time Yourself

by Peter G. Snow

If you solve this puzzle in twenty minutes, you're very smart!

Across

1 "____ I Were a Rich Man" is a popular song

3 Opposite of yes

5 Faucet (spell "pat" backwards!)

7 An animal that is supposed to be clever

8 Mechanical man

10 Opposite of peace

11 Nickname for Elizabeth

52

13 "Little Bo-peep has lost
___ sheep"

14 "Get ready; get ___;
go!"

16 A TV commercial is an

___

17 A word that sounds like
sew

Down

1 "How many miles is
___ to Babylon?"

2 A long way away

3 A negative word that
sounds like knot

4 Animal that looks like a
buffalo

6 Strength or force

7 Homes for many
soldiers

9 What a baseball player
swings

11 A place for sleeping

12 What you say when you
obey

13 A sound of laughter

15 Pussycat said: "I've
been ___ London"

30.
How Good AR You?
by Louis Sabin

As you fill in the blank spaces, cross off the words in the box on the opposite page.

#				Clue
1	A	R		"What ___ little boys made of?"
2	A	R		Barking sound from Annie's Sandy
3	A	R		Noah's boat
4	A	R		You use this to throw a ball
5	A	R		Painting or sculpture
6		A	R	Where people go to have drinks
7		A	R	Auto
8		A	R	Distant
9		A	R	Container for crackers
10		A	R	Scratch; ruin; injure
11		A	R	Golfer's score
12		A	R	Sticky substance; road cover; sailor
13		A	R	Armed conflict
14		A	R	You listen with it
15		A	R	Rower's tool
16	A		R	Breather's need

war	car	jar	tar
air	oar	are	ear
ark	par	far	art
mar	arf	arm	bar

31.
A Summer Game
by Walter Covell

As you fill the words into the puzzle, cross them out in the box on the opposite page.

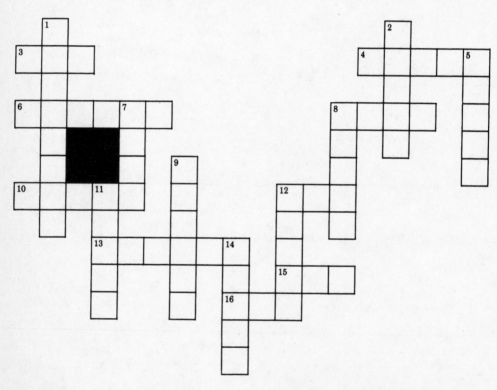

Across

3 Hit the ball with a
____.

4 ____ the ball to the batter.

6 ____ base is farthest away from the catcher.

8 The catcher wears a ____ on his face.

10 The batter stands at home ____.

12 The batter passes all the bases during a home ____.

13 A team is at bat once in each ____ .

15 A triple is a kind of ____ .

16 Three strikes make an ____ .

Down

1 Red Sox and Yankees play ____ .

2 After four balls, a batter walks to ____ base.

5 The batter who trots around all bases at once has hit a ____ .

7 When not tied, a baseball game lasts ____ innings.

8 The pitcher throws from the ____ .

9 A ____ is called when a batter swings and misses.

11 The base before home plate is ____ base.

12 The area behind first base is ____ field.

14 Each player in the field wears a ____ on one hand.

baseball	bat	first	glove
inning	mask	mound	nine
plate	right	run	second

hit	homer
out	pitch
strike	third

32.
Halloween Fun
by Bert Rosenfield

Across

1 The North Pole is ____ away

4 There is a ____ of soap in the bathroom

7 A pretty decoration on a curtain

8 Wrong names sometimes cause a ____

10 A flavor of soda

13 This outer-space fellow is in the movies

14 "What's your ____?" means "How old are you?"

15 Initials for United States

17 A place for baking

18 Elevators have ____ and downs

20 A ____ is a long way to run

23 Eat your food; don't ____ it

25 We use this for leaves on the lawn

27 In church, we ____

28 Initials for St. Louis

29 4, 6 and 8 are ____ numbers

31 If you study, you get a good ____

34 You and I

35 Chestnuts fall from a ____

36 You need ____ when you go fishing

38 At the beach you can get a nice ____

39 If you're ____ for school, you might get kept in

43 Sometimes there are ____ of people outside a movie

45 When you nod your head it means "____"

46 If you ever stepped on a banana peel, you probably ____ and fell down

47 To ____ter a room, you open the door

48 The initials for Los Angeles

50 What you do at lunchtime

59

(Continued)

51 Everybody makes
____takes

52 Most people think ice
cream is a real ____

55 On Halloween you ____
for apples

58 She rides a broomstick
on Halloween

60 This gets beaten in a
parade

62 "We ____ the World" is
a song

63 If it isn't you, it's
somebody ____

64 Never try to ____ the
traffic light

66 This animal loves the
water and is often in a
circus

68 Little insects that make
hills

69 It's black and sticky
and used to make a
road

Down

1 Mi, ____, sol

2 Highest card in the
deck

3 When the trip is over,
you ____ home

4 Like an elephant or a
dinosaur

5 This is used to chop
wood

6 To draw a straight line,
use a ____ler

7 This puzzle is a
jack-o'-____

8 You wear a ____ on
Halloween

9 This puzzle is shaped
like a ____

10 Animals that give milk

11 Shaped like an egg

12 Prince Char____ lives in
England

16 ____ Galahad was a
famous knight

19 What some children call
their father

21 Everybody must obey
the ____

22 You have one on either
side of your nose

24 December 31 is New
Year's ____

26 An ___erald is a pretty green jewel

30 Fish that are hard to hold on to

32 A handyman is ___ to do lots of jobs

33 Shower or thunderstorm

35 If the cookie ___ good, you ate it

37 Our second biggest state is ___xas

38 This means rip

40 Our biggest state is ___aska

41 The note that follows "la"

42 A short name for Edward

44 A sandwich may have a ___ of ham in it

45 If you're not quite ready, say "not ___"

49 Burned stuff belongs in the ___ can

51 This abbreviation comes after Rocky

53 One who draws pictures is an ___tist

54 The big brass instrument in the band

55 They fly on Halloween

56 "Are you coming ___ going?"

57 Good, better, ___

58 Most clothes are wash and ___

59 Not feeling good

61 Grown-up fellows

65 "___ once" means "right away"

67 An ___gle is a very big bird

33.
Pixie Puzzle
by Susan Brown

To give you a start, one word has been filled in. Can you finish the puzzle?

	1	2	3	
4 P	I	X	I	5 E
6		■	7	
8		9		
■	10			■

Across

1 This is a fluid in a tree; it's also a stupid person

4 Elf

6 Either's partner

7 Abbreviation for Los Angeles

8 Pumpkin eater in a nursery rhyme

10 Shake the head and mean "yes"

Down

1 Ambulance's noisemaker

2 Chopping tool

3 Heaped

4 "___ goes the weasel"

5 Something you hear with

9 "___ fetch a pail of water"

62

34.
The Christmas Tree

by Bert Rosenfield

Across

1 Initials for San Francisco

3 Nickname for Albert

4 What you sometimes catch a fish in

6 This is what the Three Wise Men followed

7 Iced ____ is nice in summer

8 When you play prisoner, you try to ____cape

10 The note that comes before "mi"

11 A very slippery fish

12 One Christmas song is "____lent Night"

13 A short way of writing "mountain"

14 *The ____pire Strikes Back*

16 To call your cat, you say "____, kitty"

18 If you know the answer, say "Yes, ____" (2 words)

19 Miss Muffet ____ a tuffet (2 words)

21 To drive a car, you need a ____cense

23 First two letters of the alphabet

25 They're lit on Christmas Eve

27 Rover is ____ for a dog (2 words)

29 "____ a Yankee Doodle Dandy"

30 This ____ a crossword puzzle

32 At the market, the dog ____ in the car

(Continued)

33 ___ Diego is a city in California

34 At night you go ___ bed

35 A short way of writing "street"

36 If you don't want it, say "___, thank you"

37 You open this to get inside

39 Big birds that hoot at night

Down

1 He arrives on Christmas Eve

2 This insect makes a dog scratch

5 It gets decorated on Christmas Eve

6 "We're off to ___ the Wizard"

7 A fireman ___ to put out the fire

9 This is often a Christmas present

11 He came from outer space

12 Big ___ips cross the ocean

13 "Simple Simon ___ pieman" (2 words)

15 Animal that harms a lawn when it digs a hole

17 When you're in these, you have to run

18 A big country near China

20 ___tario is in Canada

22 When somebody knocks, you say "Who ___?" (2 words)

23 Tiny bug that rhymes with can't

24 What the black sheep says

26 J, K, ___, O, P (3 letters)

27 "___ I was going to St. Ives"

28 Be ___ Valentine

31 "___ long" means "good-bye"

33 To reach a high place, you stand on this

35 A lot of ___ falls in Buffalo in the winter

37 Some dogs know how to ___ tricks

38 Initials for Ricky Schroder

35.
How Much Do You Know?

by Susan Brown

1	2	3	■	4	5	6
7			■	8		
9			10			
■		11			■	■
12	13				14	15
16			■	17		
18			■	19		

Across

1 ____ Van Winkle

4 Device for catching fish or butterflies

7 Playing card with one spot

8 Rowing tool

9 Element used in thermometers; also, a planet

11 Opposite of near

12 Person who sells plants and flowers

16 ____ conditioner

17 Large body of water

18 Major political party (Abbreviation)

19 Chick's mother

Down

1 Male sheep

2 Frozen water

3 Act

4 Feed

5 Organ of hearing

6 Attempt

10 Auto

12 Popular fashion

13 Fib

14 Look at

15 Light brown

Answers

1

2

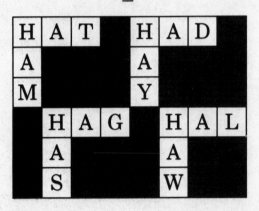

3

1. HAT
2. VAT
3. BAT
4. RAT
5. CAT

4

5

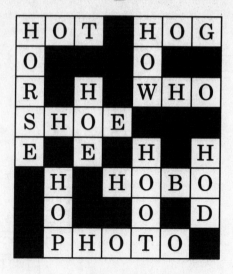

6

Clock + Hat − Cat − H = Lock

7

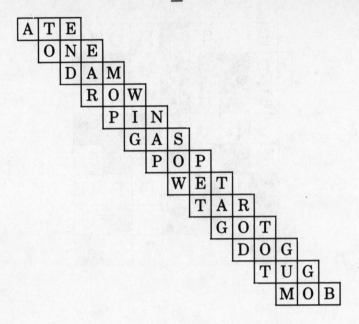

9

```
A N       H I
M O W   F A T
  D I A L S
    P I E
  S E D A N
M A D   S A T
E D     G O
```

11

G	O	N	G				G		
O			O		G	O	O	D	
A	G	O	N	Y			L		
T			D		A		D		
S		G	O	G	G	L	E	S	
	F		L		O		N		
G	O	B	A	D		G		B	
	R		I		G	O		I	
	G	O	N	E		B		N	
	O		G	O	I	N	G	O	
	T	O	G	O				O	

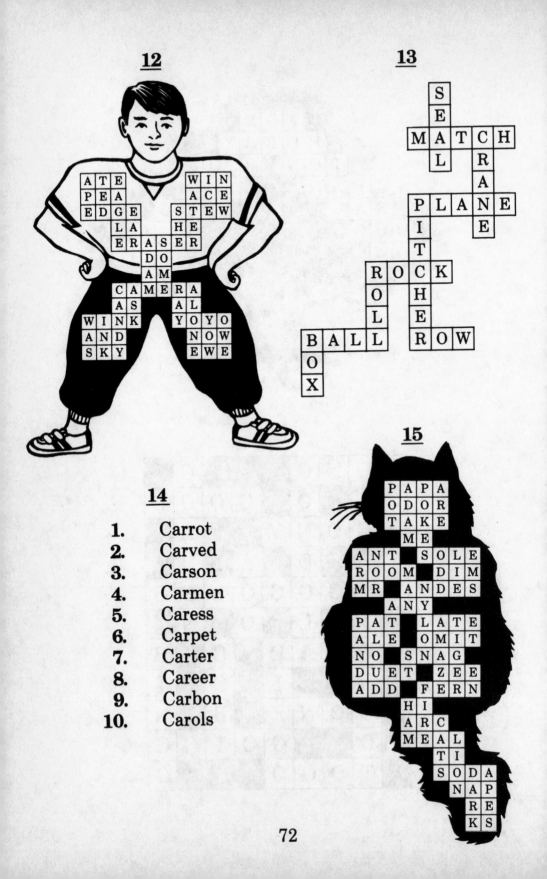

12

13

14

1. Carrot
2. Carved
3. Carson
4. Carmen
5. Caress
6. Carpet
7. Carter
8. Career
9. Carbon
10. Carols

15

16

Cone + Dog + Leg
− Egg − One = Cold

17

M I N U T E$_5$ S

M A$_9$ R C H

B A T$_8$ T E R

B O$_7$ R N

C A N$_3$ D L E S

C L O S$_6$ E T

C H I$_2$ C K E N

F I F T E E N$_4$

M$_1$ E A L

Answer: M$_1$ I$_2$ N$_3$ N$_4$ E$_5$ S$_6$ O$_7$ T$_8$ A$_9$

<u>18</u>

<u>19</u>

<u>20</u>

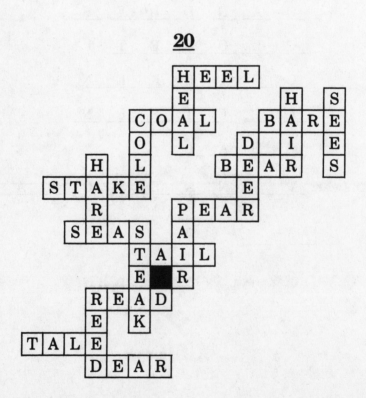

21

```
R   T A B L E           E
O         A     P O N Y E
C A S T L E   E         E
K   T   L     A
  P A W   C A R R O T
F I R E   A   O
  A     T O M A T O
  N       E   M A N
F O R K   R   I     E
L       W A T C H   S
Y A R D       E     T
```

22

```
T O M   B A D
A G O   A L E
P R O M I S E
S E N A T O R
        Y
L A B O R E R
O P E R A T E
N E T   I T S
E S S   L E T
```

23

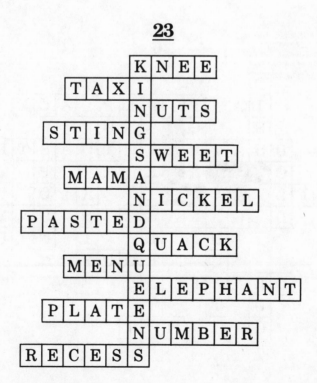

75

24

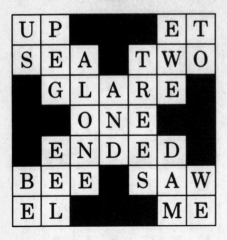

25

1. Okay
2. Joke
3. Poke
4. Woke
5. Oaks
6. Soak
7. Dock
8. Lock
9. Rock
10. Sock
11. Yolk
12. Honk
13. Cork
14. Book
15. Cook
16. Hook

26

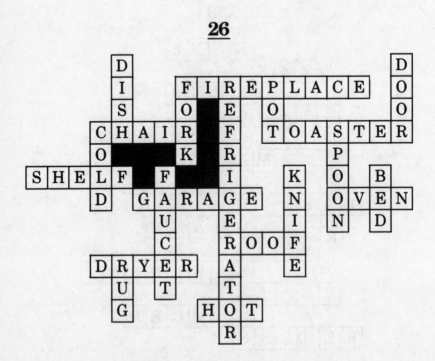

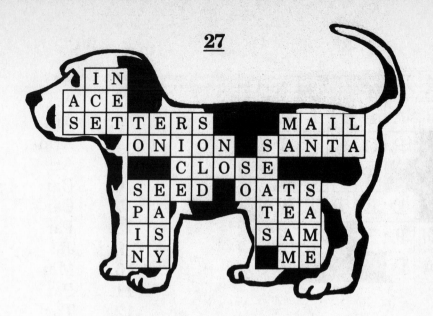

27

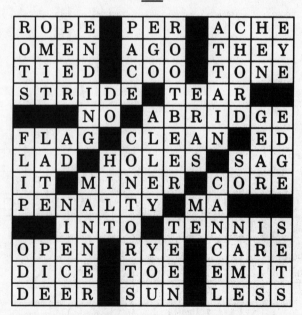

28

I	F				N	O
T	A	P		F	O	X
	R	O	B	O	T	
		W	A	R		
	B	E	T	T	Y	
H	E	R		S	E	T
A	D				S	O

30

1. Are
2. Arf
3. Ark
4. Arm
5. Art
6. Bar
7. Car
8. Far
9. Jar
10. Mar
11. Par
12. Tar
13. War
14. Ear
15. Oar
16. Air

31

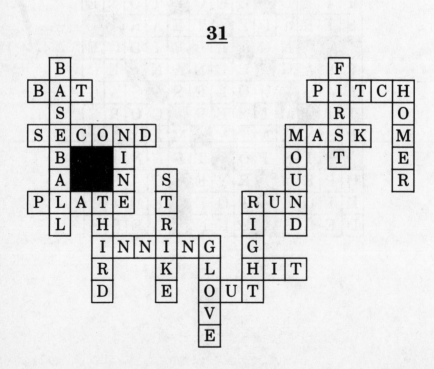

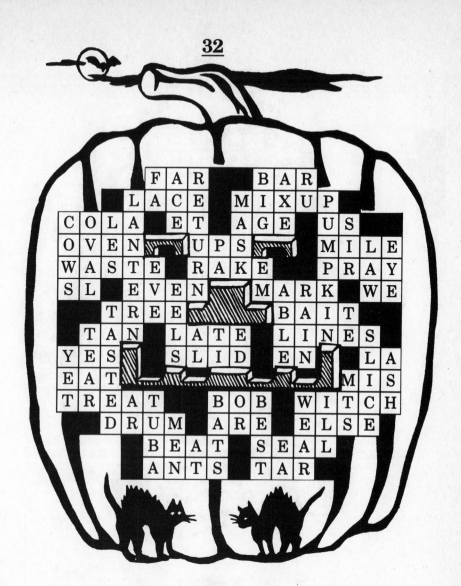